W9-AHB-020

Just A Few Friends

Just A Few Friends

Entertaining Twelve or More People

Enjoy!
Ellen Miller Coile

iUniverse, Inc.
New York Lincoln Shanghai

Just A Few Friends
Entertaining Twelve or More People and Making It Look Easy

iUniverse books may be ordered through booksellers or by contacting:

For information address:
iUniverse
2021 Pine Lake Road, Suite 100
Lincoln, NE 68512
www.iuniverse.com

ISBN-13: 978-0-595-39351-0 (pbk)
ISBN-13: 978-0-595-67698-9 (cloth)
ISBN-13: 978-0-595-83747-2 (ebk)
ISBN-10: 0-595-39351-9 (pbk)
ISBN-10: 0-595-67698-7 (cloth)
ISBN-10: 0-595-83747-6 (ebk)

Printed in the United States of America

For my best friend,
my husband,
Russell C. Coile
without whom this book
would not have been possible
...or necessary

and all my guests
without whom there
wouldn't be a party

Contents

Acknowledgments

encouraged me to write this book. That it has
to my husband, Russell C.
ddaughter,
[illegible]
Greening and her husb
daughter Courtney Coile and her husband
Zachary Coile; friends Doreen Veness; Pat Tomsett; John and
Hughes; Jude Bolan and Bill Murray; Claire and Ian Finch; Avril Nero; Rita Stiny; Tim McFadden; Joy Erler Weyer; Joanne Ryder and Lawrence Yep; Nancy and Wayne Padgett; Dolores Mollring; and numerous dinner guests over the years.

For the photographs that illustrate this book, I would like to thank my frequent dinner guests and highly skilled photographers William E. Murray, Jr., Timothy McFaddan, and Andrew C.M. Coile.

Preface

✦

The Reason Why
This Book and Called It

I grew

mother wouldn't let me try

was available. I was allowed to do a lot of the dog

like peeling potatoes or kneading bread, but nothing that would give me a feeling of accomplishment.

When I met my husband I took him home after a date and offered to fix "high tea" for him. He didn't know what that was, but readily agreed. I decided to make scrambled eggs on toast and as it was a special occasion I added a small, diced tomato to the eggs. The whole thing was a disaster! The eggs were dry and tough. I hadn't peeled the tomato so there were little bits of peel that had separated from the flesh and, of course, were inedible. The toast was so hard my husband actually broke his knife trying to cut it. Somehow, he wasn't put off by this inedible meal and proposed anyway, even though this was the only cooking I did for him before we were married. He tells everyone he married me because he knew I was such a good cook. He must have second sight because he couldn't have come to that conclusion on the evidence!

A week after we arrived in the U.S. my husband said he would like to have a few friends in for dinner. I agreed and we discussed what to have. He suggested we have a ham. As food was still rationed in England until 1954, even though the war ended in 1945, I'd never even seen a whole ham. We bought one anyway and I looked in a cook book to see how to cook it. I only had the English *Good Housekeeping Encyclopedia* and you can imagine my dismay when I read of the process to be followed: soaking it for hours, boiling for more hours (in the Washington heat) and then finally baking it. You can also imagine my joy when I discovered the people in the New World were smarter than those in the old and had thoughtfully pre-cooked the ham for me. All that was required of me was to heat it through and put a glaze of some sort on it.

Our house in the beginning was quite small so we could only manage about three couples. As the house grew, so did the guest list, until now we have a table that seats 12. I've had dinner for 50 about four times. I prefer to keep to dinners that can comfortably be seated at our ordinary dining table, i.e. 12. And that's not a bad rule for everyone. In spite of the popularity of "buffet" meals, it really is less trouble and easier to manage if people sit down at a table to eat. If your table only seats six there are ways to get other seating. For example, we set up a couple of card tables in the dining room, the conservatory and the living room. You could also use a bedroom, if necessary. In the summer, we have tables in the garden.

I think the days of my husband coming home and saying "Can we have a few friends in?" and then producing a guest list of 50 people, are over. In fact, with the escalating cost of food I have wondered if this is not the time to be writing a book telling how to feed 12 or more people. My friends have been urging me for years to write this book and now, when everything has come together—the time, the inclination, the freedom from other pressures and responsibilities it seemed like an inopportune moment, that people are having a hard enough time feeding their own families. I said as much to a friend at a party and our host

said, "Oh no, you are wrong. The harder the times the more we need our friends around us." He's right, of course, but this is a different book than the one I would have written 20 years ago. I think everyone is more concerned about the world food situation and eating less, and it could be that as we are twenty years older our friends are too and so we have all reached the stage of eating less to keep healthy. From my daughter and her friends I have learned that the young adults have a different attitude towards food than our war-and-depression genera-
[illegible] They no longer feel the need for a lavish display and, in fact,
[illegible]

ten so [illegible]
write a book I won't have to copy [illegible]
mind sharing my recipes, it's just that I get writer's cramp. Since [illegible] book was originally planned I have acquired a computer and now have many of my recipes on it, which simplifies sharing. This has not stopped the demands that I write a book because people don't feel that they can ask me for a copy of *all* my recipes.

Speaking of sharing recipes, I must tell the story a friend of mine told me once. During World War II a rather elegant lady in Virginia gave a luncheon party for her friends, including my friend. She served a casserole that was so delicious that they all asked for the recipe. She insisted that she would rather not give it and they insisted that they would really like to have it. Finally, one of the guests said that if she could produce such a delicious and nutritious dish in wartime, it was her patriotic duty to share the recipe with her friends because it would help their morale to be able to put such a dish before their families. So the hostess said, "All right. If you really want it, but don't blame me when I give it to you, as I've told you I'd rather not tell you." They really wanted it, so it was duly produced and was found to contain two cans of dog food! Well, the dogs in that county looked pretty healthy, so I don't suppose it hurt anything but their pride.

Another friend of mine told me of a relation of hers who was taken to lunch at a fashionable hotel in New York. When the waiter was clearing away their dessert dishes she said, "That was delicious. I wish I had the recipe." The waiter was very helpful and said he would see what he could do. He came back triumphantly with the recipe and handed it to her. She said, "How marvelous. Thank you very much," and he said, "That will be $100 please." She had to pay up and look big. I never heard if the recipe was really worth it and if she even tried it. It does make the cost of this book seem really nominal, doesn't it?

1

The Mechanics of It All

✦

Twelve may sound like a lot of people if you are [illegible] to cooking for two. Actually, it is harder to cater for two than twelve because you have to get the quantities right—it will be quite obvious if there is not enough of something. With 12 there is a good chance that someone will pass up the carrots or only take a token number of peas, so you can scrape through. Also, when there are 12 people to be served, the first ones tend to hold back in case things run out—they know they will be first in line for seconds anyway, so they can afford to be a bit sparing the first time around.

My husband has a horror of buffets, so we always seat people at a table. If you are living in a one-bedroom apartment you can put a card table in the bedroom, another in the living room and use your dining table. You can then rotate people between courses, if you want to, but it does get a bit confusing. I feel you need more equipment for a buffet—lots of little tables for people to put things on and everyone still needs somewhere to sit. But this is a personal preference.

You can use paper plates when you first start out but I would advise against it. Borrow, if you don't have enough—from your prospective guests, if necessary. You know that if they are eating dinner with you they won't be using their knives, forks and spoons in their own house that evening. You don't have to have 12 place settings of the finest china, but if that is your ambition, keep at it until you do. Ask for a piece each birthday, Christmas, anniversary, etc. that comes along. People will be delighted not to have to wrack their brains to think of a gift for you and will be quite sorry when your set is complete. I know. My mother-in-law collected English bone china tea cups and saucers and I was quite sad when I gave her the 12th and last. After that I had to think of something for someone who had everything, instead of just buying the prettiest cup in town. In the meantime you might find it worthwhile to get some very inexpensive dishes.

When looking for dishes, don't overlook thrift shops and consignment stores. I bought a service for 12 of fine china in a thrift shop for $100, and another for $200. A service for eight, with spares (it started as set of 12) was $45.

Having made the blanket statement that I would advise against paper plates I suppose I should state my reasons. Apart from the aesthetic one, there is the question of economics. If you are going to serve dinner on them you have to get the heavy duty ones, and they are expensive. They are used only once and then thrown away. This is bad for the pocket book as well as for the ecology. So, somehow, manage to come up with washable dishes. They don't have to match because your guests will be so amazed that you have come up with dinner for 12 in such an effortless manner that they won't notice that the dishes don't match. And if they don't, and the dinner is a flop, matching dishes wouldn't have saved the party anyway.

What is true of china, is equally true of flatware. If your ambition is to have 12 place settings of your sterling, keep at it until you do. In the meantime get something really cheap, rather than, say, silver-plate. The first time I had 50 people to dinner I borrowed flatware from some of the guests. I thought I had lost a sterling salad fork and when I looked up the price of replacing it I decided for the next party it would be more convenient and probably cheaper in the long run to buy some inexpensive stainless steel flatware. It has been used many times since—when the number of guests outnumber the pieces of silver in the family chest.

I feel the same about paper napkins as I do about paper plates. You don't have to have the finest Florentine embroidered linen—but bully [illegible] if you do! I make napkins and tablecloths from pretty, printed, [illegible] can't sew, you can fringe

[illegible]

It is nice to have [illegible]
geously expensive at the time of your party, you might [illegible]
plants in four-inch pots. I made fabric covers that I can use over and over. These plants have the advantage that they can be planted in the garden after the party. Or use house plants—ferns are always a good choice. Living in California with a convenient Farmers' Market, I can buy orchids reasonably. Remember that orchids last for three or four months, so if you average it out over the time period the cost doesn't seem so great. They are actually cheaper than cut flowers.

Or, you could try a bowl of fruit instead. Oprah is fond of saying, "A simple bowl of lemons looks wonderful." Unfortunately, a simple bowl of lemons is expensive, unless you happen to have a fecund lemon tree in the garden. A bowl of tomatoes is less expensive and you can use them—it doesn't matter that the number dwindles. Tomatoes shouldn't be kept in the refrigerator anyway, so you might as well enjoy seeing them. If you don't have a bowl that will not be in use, you can arrange the fruit on a board or even right on the table. You can offer the fruit to your guests as a final course or you can have it for your own fruit supply for the next week. If you don't intend to offer it at the end of the meal—or even if you do—you can include vegetables in the arrangement and nuts in the shell are always a good addition. Peel only the outer skin off onions and you will find a nice shiny one underneath, of a beautiful color—brown or purple depending on the variety used. Take any sad looking leaves off the outside of Brussels sprouts and use only the perfect specimens, if possible. Of course you can get by with only one good side. You can make this arrangement as large or as small as you wish. I do one about three feet long for Thanksgiving each year, but you could arrange three oranges on a few evergreen leaves with equal effect.

My Thanksgiving centerpiece takes a couple of hours to do, along with a cornucopia on the buffet. It is perfectly stable, but to be quite sure we don't have an avalanche of fruit when people sit down, I put nuts in the shell in strategic spots. More than once, an engineer type guest has spent the meal trying to determine the "key nut" only to be disappointed on removing it to find that the whole arrangement doesn't disintegrate. I bought an inexpensive door mirror to put down the middle of the table. It reflects the centerpiece and candles and protects the table.

Do have candles. You don't have to have beautiful silver candlesticks—the glow cast is just as flattering if you stick some candles in empty wine bottles, or you can drill holes in a log or board, or press a candle into the "Oasis" you use to arrange your flowers. You can also use several different styles of candlesticks of differing heights and materials with good effect.

I found, when my children were babies and joined our parties in a high chair, that they were always quieter and better behaved when there were candles on the table. So I took to lighting them every evening just for the family meals, and although they are all well past the age when they need a candle to mesmerize them into good behavior, it is a family custom that has persisted, and it is a rare evening in our house when the candles on the table are unlit. Somehow it makes every meal seem festive, and as a child of the depression I am happy to be reminded that there were times for thousands of people when there were more mealtimes than meals and give an extra little "Thank you" for the fact that we have good food for our children, ourselves and our guests.

So, someone in your family has said, "Let's have a few friends in for a meal." First, choose your guest list. The menu you select will, to some extent, be determined by the assumed appetites of your guests. For [illegible] teenage boys might be better served by lasagna or spaghetti [illegible] choose a calorie loaded

[illegible]

so the meal is [illegible]

cook, she is no good at it—so they are all experiments [illegible]

We love her anyway. Going to her house is an adventure and we keep hoping that one day she will get it right.

So, having decided on the guests, you can decide on the main course. The main thing to take into consideration is the time available for preparation. You can't slow cook roast beef if you will be out all day, but you can pop a pre-prepared lasagna into the oven to bake while you serve drinks.

Having decided on the entrée you can then select a dessert and starter. All the desserts in this book can be made ahead of time, most the day before, so you will be with your guests and not in the kitchen at the last moment.

Now you have one list with your menu, make another with all the things you will need to make it. Include everything, including coffee and the cream for it and all the things you want to offer with the drinks, plus the ingredients for the drinks. One might look like this:

Menu

Cheese
Pâté
Crackers
Nuts
Sherry

Grapefruit

Roast Beef
Peas With Thyme
Wild Rice
Gravy

Cheesecake
Coffee
Cream
Mints

Port
Cream Sherry
Walnuts

Shopping List

Roast of beef
3 packets of frozen peas
Thyme
... Rice
... Mix

Salt
4 eight-ounce pack...
Vanilla
Eggs
Cream
Coffee
Mints
Walnuts

Cheeses:
Stilton
Sharp Cheddar
Danish Blue
Brie or Camembert

Liver Pâté:
Chicken Livers
Bacon
Onions
Butter
Brandy
Port
Salt and Pepper

Crackers:
Quick Cooking Oats
Baking Soda
Butter
Salt
Woven Wheat Crackers
Cream Crackers

Drinks:
Sweet Sherry
Dry Sherry
Port
Tomato Juice
V-8 Juice
Orange Juice
Cranberry Juice

This is minutely detailed but it is worth it actually because as you make the list you can check for supplies of such things as sugar, salt, flour, butter etc. and not list them, or you can list them and check off the things you have. Items like butter are listed each time they occur in a recipe so that you can be sure you have enough total for your needs.

Buy as much ahead of time as possible. The drinks can certainly be bought well in advance as long as you are sure no one will drink them! You could put a "hands off" sign on them, if in doubt. The peas, wild rice, gravy mix, coffee, mints can all be purchased well in advance. I get these things taken care of as soon as possible after I've decided to have a party. They can be bought along with the family groceries and this method has the salutary effect of spreading the cost out and so making [illegible] expense of a party seem minimal.

[illegible] party, Thursday for a Saturday do, you [illegible] have everything

deciding [illegible]

If you really put a lot of time [illegible]

early in the week and check it out. You don't want to [illegible] thing only to find at the last minute it has a button missing or the hem down. The secret of making entertaining easy is good planning and then being relaxed about it if the unexpected happens. You want to be like a duck, calm and serene on the surface but paddling like mad underneath. If something does go wrong in spite of all your efforts, shrug it off, it isn't the end of the world. And remember, the people around that table are your friends and the same thing, or worse, has probably happened to them sometime and so they feel for you.

Although my husband doesn't like to eat buffet style, balancing a plate on his knee, I always serve buffet style. If you have 12 or more people at the table and serve in the usual way, by the time you have served meat and two vegetables to everyone the food will be stone cold. I have two "Hot Trays" and go to a lot of trouble to serve the hot food hot and the cold food cold, and I don't want people to sit politely waiting for everyone to be served while the meal goes cold. I explain that I serve buffet style and ask people to come and serve themselves at the beginning of the meal and that it is a house rule to eat as soon as you have collected your food from the buffet. The method of serving buffet style and sitting at a table is a perfect compromise as far as I am concerned. In practice I have found that the first person to be served usually waits until someone else nearby is served so that they won't be eating alone. It is only the main course that is served this way. The first course is already in place when guests are called to the table. I serve dessert from the end of the table or the buffet and pass it round. Coffee is poured and taken round by me unless one of my children happens to be present and volunteers for the job.

I've found recently, among our liberated friends, both male and female, that they prefer to forget the "ladies first" rule and just go in any order that suits. If you have a guest of honor, they can be invited to come to the buffet first. I think "ladies first" was a plot by men to make sure they didn't have cold food! Just kidding! Actually, I grew up in a poor family where the men, as the bread winners, were always served first. They had to have enough food to stay healthy to continue working to support the family—in those days, no work, no pay. When we first started entertaining I had to remind myself before each party to serve the ladies first, rather like the captain of the ship who looked in a locked drawer from time to time. When someone finally got a look inside they found it contained only a piece of paper with the legend "Starboard—Right; Port—Left."

This reminds me of a story a friend of ours told of visiting Africa. His hostess had a new maid she had been training and the dinner party he was at was to be her debut. He was standing near the kitchen and he heard the anxious instruction "Now remember, serve from the left and clear from the right." To which the maid replied, under her breath, "And they say we're superstitious!"

2

Welcome Aboard

◆

going to serve them a meal. [illegible]
even more than one couple, they won't all arrive at the same time. So, even if you would like to, you can't rush them into the dining room and waiting meal the moment they arrive, and you can't have them just standing around twiddling their thumbs. The best thing to do is to put a glass in one hand and something to eat in the other.

For years our house was "dry" but we now serve wine. Under the circumstances, I'm not going to give you recipes for fabulous cocktails, or rum punch or anything like that—I'm sure you have all you want. When our guests arrive we offer them a glass of sherry or white wine but during the dry years there were several drinks we used to greet people that were relished by our guests. So, if you are hard up financially when some party presents itself, or you prefer not to serve alcohol, you might find these a good way to welcome guests.

Tangy Tomato V-8

1 large can V-8 juice
¼ cup lemon juice (or slices of lemon to float on punch)
2 teaspoons Worcestershire sauce
4 dashes Angostura bitters

Combine ingredients in saucepan. Heat. Serve hot.

Tomato Bisque Soup

Another good welcome on a cold and frosty evening is tomato bisque soup with a spoonful of sour cream on the top. Serve in a mug and hand each guest a soup spoon at the same time.

Mulled Cider

1 gallon cider
Two whole cinnamon sticks
12 whole cloves

Combine ingredients in a saucepan. Heat. Serve hot.

And for hot weather nothing beats Cranberry-Apple Fizz.

Cranberry-Apple Fizz

Have all ingredients chilled.

2 cups cranberry juice

2 cups apple juice

1 tablespoon lemon juice (or lemon slices to float)

... ginger ale

... cranberry

I never get worked up ...
before a meal. But a lot of people, including me, ...
an empty stomach. So the lazy or relaxed solution is a cheese tray. It is very easy to have, say, a blue cheese, Cheddar, Gouda or Edam and Brie attractively arranged with some crackers. If you really want to impress people with all the trouble you have taken, include some of your home baked Oat Cakes with the crackers.

Oat Cakes

1 cup Quick Cooking oats
Pinch of baking soda
½ teaspoon salt
1 tablespoon bacon fat or butter
Boiling water

Mix dry ingredients. Melt fat with 1 tablespoon water and pour into the center. Mix to a soft consistency, adding boiling water as required. Turn onto a floured board, knead lightly. Roll out thinly and cut into fingers or shapes (I prefer mine round, for some reason). Place on a floured cookie sheet and bake at 375° for 20 to 30 minutes, or until crisp and lightly browned.

Oat cakes can also be eaten for breakfast with bacon and egg, etc. I make up several batches of the "mix" and store them in individual plastic boxes so that it is no trouble just to melt the butter and make up a batch. I would make a double batch for a dinner party of 12—they keep very well in an air tight container.

In my family Oat Cakes are affectionately known as "Wee Boards" because of the following story told to us by a friend. A Scottish lady went to live in Dublin and one day a neighborhood child came and asked her for some bread and jam. She had run out of bread so she put some jam on an Oat Cake and gave it to him. After a while there was another knock on the door and the small boy appeared and said, "Thanks very much for the jam, missus. And here's your wee board back." I should point out that the home made ones bear no relation to the wee boards that pass for oat cakes when you buy them in a store.

You might also find Cheese Wafers handy because they, too, can be made up ahead of time.

Cheese Wafers

½ pound grated sharp cheese
1 stick butter, creamed
1 ½ cups sifted flour
Heavy pinch cayenne pepper
½ teaspoon salt

butter, salt and pepper. Add flour. Mix

I've never managed to keep any around for a month, so I'm taking that bit on trust! Actually, if you put them in an airtight container in a cool place, you can make them and they will keep for a month, which is what I do.

Now with the cheese tray, a bowl of olives and a dish of nuts, it might be nice to put out some liver Pâté. This couldn't be easier to make, if you have a blender, and the great thing about it is that it freezes very well. I make up a big batch and then have it in the freezer for emergencies. Sort of frozen assets.

Liver Pâté

6 ounces chicken livers
3 strips bacon
1 small onion
1 stick + 2 tablespoons butter
3 teaspoons brandy
3 teaspoons port
Salt and pepper to taste

Cut the bacon into pieces, peel and chop the onion. Lightly fry the bacon, add the onion and chicken livers. Cook lightly for about five minutes. Use a little of the butter if the bacon hasn't produced enough fat. Put the contents of the frying pan into a blender. Add the butter, brandy, port and freshly ground pepper and blend until smooth. Turn into freeze proof dishes and keep until needed.

3

To Start the Meal

✦

I happen to think there

Or end one, for that matter.

One of the easier things to have is half a grapefruit. Do cut around the outside and run the knife along each side of the dividing membrane so that the guests don't either have to fight to get at the meat or run the risk of a shower bath while attacking it, with juice spurting everywhere. I must confess to not being overly fond of those special spoons with a serrated tip—they are only marginally easier to use than an ordinary spoon, and it only takes a moment to fix a grapefruit. I've done it for fifty and it really wasn't that big a deal.

The nice thing about serving grapefruit is that you can do it all ahead of time—if you haven't got room to put all the bowls in the refrigerator, put the bowls in place on the table, then put the prepared grapefruit on a tray in the refrigerator and put them in the bowls just before you call people to the table.

The second easiest thing to serve to start a meal is melon. Cantaloupe is super served with a wedge of lime. Put the melon wedge in the bowl. Run a knife along the rind and then cut the loosened fruit once or twice lengthways then across at intervals to make bite size pieces. This also saves a struggle with the spoon and will make your guests feel you have gone the second mile for them.

A little more trouble, but only just, is a fresh fruit salad. I've gained a reputation over the years for my fruit salad but there is really nothing to it. I've often wondered if it seems better than some because I don't feel the need to jazz it up with Kirsch or anything else alcoholic for that matter. The greater the variety in a fruit salad the more fun, but you can make a passable fruit salad in the dead of winter with, say, bananas, which always seem to be available, and apples and a small can of mandarin orange slices. If you have only white fruit it is a good idea to include either oranges or frozen raspberries or strawberries to give it some color and a little change of texture.

You can include in your fruit salad any or all of the following fruits: apples, pears, bananas, pineapple (fresh or canned), melon (any variety, including watermelon), strawberries and raspberries (fresh or frozen), oranges (any kind, including canned), cherries (if you want to appear to have taken special care, de-pit them), grapes (cut in half and deseeded if necessary, whole if seedless), canned grapefruit segments, cut up plums, etc. If you live in an exotic place, like the tropics, I am sure there are other things like papayas and mangoes and in Italy we added several varieties of persimmons. Peaches are also good—don't peel them unless absolutely necessary for some odd reason. The skins add color to the dish and necessary roughage to the diet.

A fruit salad can either be put into little bowls just before guests are called to the table, as with the grapefruit, or it can be served in a glass dish and passed around.

If you are having a very informal party—say a spaghetti supper on the patio, you could start with big wedges of watermelon to be eaten in the traditional manner, with a big bowl conveniently placed for people to spit the seeds—otherwise you may find yourself living in a watermelon patch the following season!

I seldom think of serving soup at a dinner party, for some reason, but if I do I serve cream of chicken soup with a blob of sweet whipped or sour cream on the top and just a shake of paprika on the top of the cream for color. It really is delicious.

So now we have everyone seated and the meal started, we are well on our way.

4

The Main Course

✦

me the easiest thing in the [illegible] tenderloin, cooked as a roast. It may look more expensive in the store, but there is so little waste that I believe it to be the cheapest meat in the long run. It is also fool proof. I have never had a tenderloin that wasn't wonderful. It is also delightfully easy to serve. This is for a really elegant meal—there are less formal meals I will also cover.

We have never minded having roast beef left over. In fact we don't call it leftover—it is planned-over. You can slice it for supper or use it for roast beef sandwiches. You can even grind it and make a cottage pie, but that seems like a waste of tenderloin. So I tend to cook a larger roast than I think I will need, or two smaller ones, and it never goes amiss. About four ounces per person for a boneless cut is about right.

I use the slow cooking method for all meats except ham or pork. Preheat oven to 375°. Brush roast all over with oil. Put in hot oven for one hour. Reduce temperature to 150°–250°. The length of cooking time is a bit hard to tell because it depends on whether or not you have put the meat in frozen (I always do) and how thick it is. You will have to play it by ear a bit, but a good meat thermometer is absolutely essential for this method of cooking if you are not to serve still frozen or raw meat or ruin it by over cooking. For a roast for the evening meal I aim to have it in the oven by two o'clock. If you are a bit later you can still do it, but you will have to have the temperature at the higher end of the range mentioned above. If you want the meat well done or for lamb, you can put it in the oven after washing the breakfast dishes and forget about it until the evening, having reduced the temperature to 150° after the first hour at 375°. With the beef that you want to serve rare, however, you will need a bit more attention to how it is doing. As soon as it has defrosted, put the meat thermometer in. This will usually be after the first couple of hours (an hour after you turned the heat down). When you put the thermometer in you will see how low it goes, or if it races up towards where you want it to end. Then you can adjust the heat of the oven accordingly. This all sounds very unscientific, and I suppose it is, but if you try it with just the family roast a couple of times you will soon get the hang of it and you will be able to serve perfect roast beef every time. The main advantages of this method of cooking is that the meat doesn't shrink in the cooking and if you want medium rare roast beef the whole of the roast will be medium rare all the way through, not just in the middle but all the way to the edges of each slice and from the outside to the inside.

With roast beef for a party I don't attempt to have potatoes. I usually serve plain boiled rice. I am fortunate to have a Chinese rice cooker which takes the work and worry out of rice cooking. But I also serve wild rice, all with gravy. I'll discuss the second vegetable later because it is common to all the main dishes.

If you would like to serve beef and think roast beef too costly, Beef Stroganoff is another possibility. Maybe this isn't cheaper, but it certainly seems so, because you need less meat per person—about three ounces instead of four ounces.

Beef Stroganoff

1 ½ pounds tenderloin
1 pound mushrooms, peeled and cut in large pieces
2 cups chopped onions
1 pint sour cream
...ns corn or olive oil

... with the flat

When the mushroo...
cream and season to taste. Keep it warm bu...
with buttered noodles.

I know there are Beef Stroganoff recipes using cheaper meat, even hamburger, but this is the real thing! However, for Hamburger Stroganoff, see Chapter Six on Lunch and Supper.

If you are cutting down on red meat you might try "the other white meat" with Pork Stroganoff.

Pork Stroganoff

1 ½ pounds pork tenderloin
2 tablespoons butter
1 tablespoon olive oil
2 onions, thinly sliced
Half a pound of mushrooms, thinly sliced
Salt and freshly ground black pepper
2 tablespoons gin
12 ounces sour cream
Minced parsley
Paprika

Remove any unsightly fat or outer skin from the pork. Slice across the grain into rounds about a quarter inch thick. Heat half the oil and butter in a large frying pan until sizzling. Fry half the pork briskly to brown on both sizes, about three minutes. Transfer to a plate with a slotted spoon. Cook the other half of the pork in the same way.

Add the rest of the butter and oil to the pan and cook the onions gently until soft, then add the mushrooms and continue to cook gently, turning them over until the juices run. Season with a little salt and lots of pepper. Remove the pan contents to another plate.

Return the pork rounds to the pan, heat gently and pour the gin over the meat. Let it warm up for two minutes, then set fire to it and baste until the flames die out. Add the onions and mushrooms, stir in the sour cream and bring to a bubbling simmer. Check seasoning.

Sprinkle with minced parsley and a good pinch of paprika. Serve immediately over hot buttered noodles or plain boiled rice.

We like to have this leftover, so I always cook a double batch. It also freezes beautifully. It can be made one or two days in advance to let the flavors meld.

Hungarian Goulash

4 pounds beef chuck or round steak cut into 1 inch cubes
¼ cup shortening

1 teaspoon dry mustard
Dash red pepper
3 cups water
¼ cup flour
¼ cup cold water

Brown beef in hot shortening. Add onions and garlic; cook and stir until onion is tender. Mix ketchup and seasonings; add to skillet and stir. Add three cups water; cover and simmer for two to two and a half hours (or use a pressure cooker). Blend flour and ½ cup cold water; stir into meat mixture. Heat to boiling, stirring constantly.

While Hungarian Goulash is delicious, just as good and not nearly as much trouble, especially if you have a pressure cooker, is Beef in Burgundy.

Beef in Burgundy

4 pounds beef chuck or bottom round cut into 1 inch cubes
¼ cup olive or corn oil
2 packets French Onion Soup mix
Burgundy or other red wine

Brown beef in hot oil. Add onion soup mix. Pour in enough Burgundy to come just over half way up the meat. Bring up to pressure and cook for half an hour. If you do not have a pressure cooker, simmer on low heat or in oven for two to two and a half hours or until tender, adding more Burgundy as needed. You can also put this in a crock pot and cook for about 12 hours on low. Serve with buttered noodles, or rice if you prefer.

This next recipe for Italian Tomato Sauce will be a mainstay for both entertaining and for your family meals. It freezes beautifully, so I always make a double recipe and freeze any left over in amounts just right for a family meal. You know how large your family is and so how much that will be.

Italian Tomato Sauce

2 large cans tomato puree (1 pound 12 ounces each)
2 small cans tomato paste (6 ounces each)
1 ½ cups water
6 tablespoons olive oil (3 fluid ounces)
3 teaspoons garlic salt
[illegible]

Combine all ingredients listed above. [illegible]
for at least half an hour. Add water if sauce becomes too thick.

Italian Meat Sauce

Make the tomato sauce as above. While it simmers, brown two pounds ground round or ground chuck in a skillet. Drain off fat and add the meat to the sauce.

Serve with boiled spaghetti. Pass grated Parmesan cheese to sprinkle on top. Don't tell the Italians, but this is just as good with rice, if you prefer it.

Italian Meat Balls

2 slices of bread, each 1-inch thick, soaked in water, milk or stock to cover
3 pounds ground meat (either all beef or a mixture of beef, veal and pork)
4 eggs, beaten
2 tablespoons butter
½ cup minced onion
6 tablespoons chopped parsley (3 fluid ounces)
1 tablespoon salt
½ teaspoon paprika
1 clove garlic, minced
3 tablespoons grated Parmesan cheese
½ teaspoon oregano

Put the meat in a bowl. Add the beaten eggs. Melt the butter in a skillet and sauté the onions until golden. Add them to the meat. Wring the liquid from the bread and add it to the meat with the parsley, salt, paprika, garlic, oregano and cheese. Mix thoroughly and then form into balls. Brown lightly in four tablespoons butter. Place browned meatballs in a casserole and half cover with tomato sauce, as above. Bake covered for about 30 minutes.

Another good way to use this sauce is in Lasagna. Use the tomato sauce with meat added. This also freezes very well but be sure you defrost it completely before reheating, otherwise you will more than likely find ice crystals in the middle when you go to serve it. It takes a long time to defrost too—about three days in the refrigerator or a day at room temperature, which probably explains why it is so hard to heat it through from the frozen state in the oven. If in doubt, insert your meat thermometer to check.

Lasagna

1 pound lasagna noodles
4 eggs
½ pound mozzarella cheese

Filling: mix together ricotta, [illegible] meg and salt and pepper to taste. Arrange in layers in a large baking dish, starting with sauce on bottom of pan, then lasagna, filling, lasagna, sauce, lasagna, filling, lasagna, sauce. Sprinkle top with parmesan cheese. Bake for 40 minutes at 375°. This serves 12 small appetites. If you have teenagers or big eaters, make two.

This can be served as is, or one pound of ground beef can be browned and added to the sauce.

Vegetarian Lasagna

For vegetarian lasagna, cut up half a pound of mushrooms and sauté them in a little butter or olive oil and add to the sauce. Cook as above.

This reminds me of the time we were invited to have dinner at the home of an Admiral whose wife was well known for a series of small cookbooks of the "make it now, eat it later" type. I was really looking forward to it. "Boy, are we going to get some meal—she being a cookbook author and all," I told my husband. I was invited to serve myself first and as I put the spoon into the casserole there was a loud crunch of ice crystals. We just smiled and ate it, but she heard it too. The salad was very good!

Another easy main dish that needs no recipe from me is a whole ham. This is another thing we don't mind having left over as we like ham sandwiches and I use the bones for making thick pea soup which is a meal in itself. Then I cut up the small bits for use in quiche which I will discuss under "lunches." It's nice to have a little pile of ham all ready in the freezer with another pile of pastry cases ready for a quick meal.

As all hams seem to be sold pre-cooked these days the only thing that needs to be done is to be sure it is heated through. The easiest way to dress it up is to add pineapple slices and mandarin oranges in an attractive design half an hour before you wish to serve it. Stick some whole cloves in the pineapple for extra flavor. Serve with candied sweet potatoes. I use canned ones and just add the butter and brown sugar before heating them in the oven. Or I use fresh ones that I bake in their jackets, like white potatoes.

I suppose one of the easiest meals to cook is a turkey dinner. You will have your own traditional things to go with it but I serve sweet potatoes and white ones and always Brussels sprouts and chestnuts as the vegetable. I use herb-seasoned stuffing mix using the recipe on the package with an egg in it.

I always put the bird in the oven the night before I want to serve it.

Roast Turkey

Stuff in the usual way. Preheat oven to 375°. Put bird in covered roaster or cover with foil. Put in hot oven and cook for one hour. Lower heat to 150°. The nicest thing about this method is waking up on Christmas morning and finding the house full of the delicious aroma of cooking turkey and not having to jump out of bed at the crack of dawn to get the bird in the oven in time for dinner before midnight. When you go downstairs put a meat thermometer in the bird and if it seems a bit low for when you want to serve, raise the temperature to 200°. An hour before you want to serve, take the bird from the oven, raise the temperature to 375°. When the oven is hot, take the foil off the turkey and put the bird back in the oven, basting it well before you do. Cook for one hour, basting every 15 minutes, and the bird will be a rich dark brown.

I use turkey gravy mix, but use the juice from the bird for part of the liquid.

I always buy a large bird because we don't like to have to skimp on turkey sandwiches afterwards (have you tried putting cranberry jelly or sauce in them instead of mustard?). I am the only one in my family that likes the dark meat so unless we have had a number of guests who also like it there is a lot left over. I used to have a hard time using it up until I got the bright idea of making a curry out of it. The family loves it. Serve cranberry sauce with the curry too.

Now we come to that near relation of the turkey—chicken. You probably have your own favorite ways of serving it. Here are mine.

Chicken Cacciatore

Three 4 pound chickens, cut into individual pieces, or use chicken breasts, one half per person
½ cup flour
¼ cup olive oil
6 tablespoons chopped onions or onion flakes (3 fluid ounces)
3 cloves garlic, crushed
¾ cup Italian tomato paste

6 tablespoons brandy (3 fluid ounces)
¼ teaspoon marjoram

Dredge the chicken with the flour. Sauté until golden brown in olive oil with the onions (not the flakes) and garlic. Mix the rest of the ingredients together. Add to the chicken. Simmer covered for an hour or until tender. Serve with boiled spaghetti.

This is a really easy recipe because you don't even have to brown the chicken first and is a good dish to make the day before you want to serve it because it is even better if it has a chance to "age" and the flavor permeates the chicken.

Chinese Soy Chicken

2 ½ cups soy sauce
3 tablespoons honey
1 ½ cups brown sugar
4 ½ cups water
6 tablespoons sherry (3 fluid ounces)
6 tablespoons chopped fresh ginger* (3 ounces) (or 3 teaspoons ground ginger)
9 cloves garlic, crushed
3 star anise* (or ½ teaspoon fennel seeds)
¾ cup green onions cut in ½ inch lengths

Mix the ingredients in a large saucepan. Bring to a boil and simmer two minutes. Add three 4 pound frying chickens cut into individual pieces including livers and gizzards, or use chicken breasts, one half per person, with a few extras in case anyone wants seconds. Simmer 40 minutes or until tender. Serve with boiled rice and the sauce the chicken was cooked in.

* Star anise can be bought at Chinese grocery stores. So can fresh ginger which is also usually available at ordinary grocery stores. If you find it you can always put some in the freezer, although it keeps weeks just in the crisper of the refrigerator. I chop all the ginger when I first get it and then freeze it in the sherry in measured amounts for one recipe.

If you liked the above touch of Chinese but want a cookout try Chinese Barbequed Chicken.

Chinese Barbequed Chicken

3 ready to cook chickens, cut up, or use chicken breasts
12 tablespoons soy sauce
6 teaspoons sugar
6 cloves garlic
3 teaspoons spices of 5 fragrances
6 tablespoons salad oil (3 fluid ounces)

often. Serve with plain boiled rice.

Here is another easy recipe which can be made the day before.

Chicken Supreme

6 whole chicken breasts
2 cans Cream of Chicken soup
½ cup Sour Cream
1 pound mushrooms, peeled and cut into large pieces
2 cups chopped onions
2 tablespoons dry sherry
3 tablespoons corn oil
4 to 6 chicken bouillon cubes

Simmer chicken breasts until tender in bouillon made with cubes. Cool. Sauté onions in hot oil until just transparent, add mushrooms and cook a little longer.

Remove from heat. Add chicken soup and sour cream. Remove chicken from bones, discard skin, and cut meat into bite size pieces. Add to rest of ingredients. Just heat through. Do not boil. If made the day before be careful not to boil on reheating. Serve over boiled rice or noodles.

Another nice easy chicken recipe which is a family favorite with us is

Chicken Americana

3 ready to cook chickens, cut up, or use chicken breasts
2 sticks butter, melted
1 tablespoon salt
1 ¼ teaspoons pepper
1 ½ teaspoons garlic salt
1 ½ cups herb-seasoned stuffing mix

Preheat oven to 350°. Arrange chicken pieces, one layer deep and skin side up in a shallow baking dish, close together so the pieces touch. Pour the melted butter over the chicken. Sprinkle with the salt, pepper and garlic powder, then with the stuffing crumbs. Bake uncovered until fork tender, about I ¾ hours.

I usually serve jacket-baked potatoes with this as they cook while the chicken is cooking. I put a skewer or spike in the potatoes so they are done in the same time. If yours usually take longer you could put them in while you are getting the chicken ready.

With this I serve peach halves with a teaspoon of chutney in the middle, either heated in the oven at the end of the cooking time or placed under the broiler until brown and bubbly. I also serve these with leg of lamb or lamb curry. Or use Cranberry Port Chutney—see recipe under "Chutneys."

Having mentioned leg of lamb I suppose I may as well continue with it. This is slow cooked like the roast beef but is put in right after

I am not among

Shrimp in Wine

6 tablespoons flour
1 tablespoon salt
¾ teaspoon pepper
4 ½ to 5 pounds uncooked shrimp, shelled and cleaned
6 tablespoons olive oil (3 fluid ounces)
2 ½ cups dry white wine
6 tablespoons Italian tomato paste (3 fluid ounces)
6 tablespoons boiling water (3 fluid ounces)
6 spring onions chopped, both white and green part
3 tablespoons chopped parsley

Combine the flour, salt and pepper on a piece of wax paper. Toss the shrimp in the mixture.

Heat the oil in a skillet and lightly brown the shrimp on both sides. Stir together the wine, tomato paste, water and onion. Add to shrimp. Cook over low heat stirring occasionally.

Sprinkle with the chopped parsley. Taste for seasoning. Serve with boiled rice.

Vegetables

I'm afraid I don't put too much effort into vegetables when we entertain. For most of the main dishes I have listed and the lunch dishes that follow later, the best thing to serve with them is a nice tossed green salad. The one exception is the ham, and with it I would have

Pineapple Coleslaw

1 head white cabbage
1 small can pineapple tidbits
1 cup mayonnaise

Shred the cabbage very fine. Cut the pineapple tidbits in half if they seem too big, drain and add to the cabbage. Stir in the mayonnaise. Add a little of the pineapple juice if necessary and a little more mayonnaise if needed.

Tossed Green Salad

As much Iceberg, Romaine and Boston lettuce as needed, depending on whether you have all three or only one variety, torn into fairly large pieces..

6 small, 3 large or 24 cherry tomatoes, cut into wedges but not peeled

... sliced thin

them and ...

feel strongly about serving them, may I suggest a separate dish placed next to the salad bowl?

As you can see I have suggested leaving everything in fairly large (but bite size) pieces as it ruins greens to be chopped up small. In fact, a lettuce grower told me you should never cut lettuce—you should always tear it. If you cut lettuce and put it in the refrigerator it will turn brown where cut, but it won't brown at the tear.

As well as a salad or coleslaw you could serve Green Beans Almondine.

Green Beans Almondine

Nothing could be simpler. Use either fresh, frozen or canned beans. When I use the latter I use whole green beans, three cans, drained, in a casserole with a tiny bit of the liquid and chopped almonds sprinkled over the top. They just need to be heated through, so if you are serving roast beef, for example, you can put them covered in the oven with the meat. As an alternative, you can add a can of mushroom soup diluted with half a can of milk to the beans and put the almonds on the top.

I suppose frozen peas are the housewife's friend as they are always available and are easy to cook. For a change try Peas with Thyme.

Peas with Thyme

3 packages frozen peas
1 teaspoon salt
1 teaspoon dried thyme
1 tablespoon butter
½ cup water

Place frozen peas in a microwaveable dish. Add salt, thyme, and butter. Cook until peas are just tender. You can get this all ready early in the day and then microwave just before you want to serve the peas.

For special occasions, especially Thanksgiving and Christmas, we have Brussels Sprouts and Chestnuts.

Brussels Sprouts and Chestnuts

1 pound chestnuts
2 teaspoons salt
4 packages frozen Brussels sprouts (or equivalent fresh)

tender, about ten minutes. Drain. [illegible]
nuts. Add melted butter and seasonings. Alternatively, you can cook them in the microwave, a few at a time. Be sure to slit the shells or they will explode.

I sometimes serve buttered carrots but usually stick to a green vegetable. When in season, nothing is nicer than asparagus with Italian dressing. Actually, broccoli is just as good as asparagus with dressing on it. In fact, my youngest son puts dressing on all greens, including plain boiled cabbage, and why not?

5

Dessert

l walnuts.

You do...
are easy to do, never fail, can be made ...
before and are really good. So here are my favorites.

I have never met a foreigner who likes pumpkin pie. Some say, when questioned, "Oh, I don't mind it" or words to that effect but when questioned further, in over fifty years I have only met one who said he would order it in a restaurant, but it would depend on what else was on the menu. I dislike it so much that I won't cook it. There are very few items of food I don't enjoy and even fewer that I can't get down. Pumpkin pie is one, and citrus peel in any form is another. This has always rather distressed me as I feel it underlines my "mid-Atlantic, treading water right in the middle" status, because I obviously will never be a true American if I can't eat the national dish of pumpkin pie, and I certainly can't have been a true Englishwoman, being unable to have marmalade and toast for breakfast! But there it is.

So on occasions when other true blue American families are tucking into pumpkin pie our polygenetic lot are having what I tell myself is an equally traditional dish instead.

Pecan Pie

3 eggs
¾ cup brown sugar
1 cup dark corn syrup
1 stick butter
1 cup pecans
1 unbaked 9-inch pie shell

Beat eggs until light. Blend in brown sugar. Slowly stir in melted butter. Blend thoroughly. Add corn syrup. Beat until well mixed. Add ½ cup pecans. Turn into pie shell. Sprinkle remaining pecans (whole, if possible) on top. Bake at 300° for an hour or until knife inserted in custard comes out clean. Serve with whipped cream if desired. You'll need two of these for twelve people.

Walnut Pie

Another family favorite is Walnut Pie. The recipe is the same as Pecan Pie except that the nuts are different. As walnuts are less sweet than pecans this pie is less sweet, which many people prefer.

This next dish is a never fail, guaranteed success, and can be made the day before.

Cheese Cake

1 ½ cups Graham cracker crumbs
2 tablespoons butter
2 tablespoons sugar

Melt butter. Mix the sugar with the cracker crumbs, blend in but-
[illegible] mixture into bottom of a 9-inch spring form pan.

[illegible]
1 cup cream

Blend sugar with flour, salt and cream cheese softened at room temperature. Add vanilla. Add egg yolks, one at a time, mixing well after each yolk is added. Add cream, blend thoroughly. Fold in stiffly beaten egg whites. Pour mixture on top of crumb base. Bake in a slow moderate oven (325°) for one hour or until set in center. Cool before removing rim of pan.

I always make two cheesecakes for twelve people. I like to be able to offer second helpings but if it doesn't get touched, it freezes beautifully and you can add it to your frozen assets—it's like money in the bank, and on occasion, a lot more convenient.

You can put a fruit glaze over this cheesecake if you want to but it really isn't necessary as it is delicious without it.

Another excellent cake, which is best made the day before so it can "mature," is Rum Cake.

Rum Cake

1 package (4 serving size) yellow cake mix
1 package Vanilla Instant pudding and pie filling
4 eggs
½ cup cold water
½ cup corn oil
½ cup dark rum

…il and rum in

¾ cup sugar
½ cup butter
¼ cup water
½ cup dark rum

Combine ingredients in a saucepan. Bring to a boil and boil five minutes. Remove from heat and stir in rum. Remove cake from pan onto serving plate. Prick with cake tester or skewer. Spoon warm glaze over warm cake, slowly allowing the glaze to sink into the cake. As the cake usually comes apart on top, you can pour part of the glaze into the crevasse before turning the cake out onto the serving plate.

Chocolate Rum Cake

This cake is the same as above, using a chocolate cake mix and chocolate instant cake mix.

And if you are really cake people and "chocoholics" (like me) you could try Cocoa Cake.

Cocoa Cake

2 cups flour (stir to aerate before measuring)
2 cups sugar
1 cup unsweetened cocoa
1 cup water
1 cup sour cream
¼ cup butter, softened
½ teaspoon baking powder
1 ¼ teaspoons baking soda
1 teaspoon salt
2 eggs
1 teaspoon vanilla

In a large mixer bowl, mix all ingredients in order given. Blend at low speed ½ minute, scraping bowl constantly, then beat at high speed three minutes longer, scraping bowl often.

Turn into greased and floured 12x9x2 inch pan. Bake in preheated 350° oven until cake tester inserted in center comes out clean, 35 to 40 minutes. Cool on wire rack. Cut in pan and remove as needed.

This is so delicious it doesn't need frosting but you can if you want to. You could serve it with a dab of whipped cream or with ice cream.

If you are having a heavy meal and would like a light dessert to end try Chocolate Mousse.

Chocolate Mousse

12 ounces semi-sweet chocolate chips
¼ cup (preferably sweet) sherry or rum

evening meal or the day before.

If you are lucky enough to have a copper bowl for whipping your egg whites you will get more servings out of this recipe than if you don't. It really does make a difference but it is not overly important if you don't happen to have one.

Having told you how to have a light dessert I am going to tell you what you can have with it if, instead of the ladies sewing circle that you were expecting, every last one of which is on a diet, you suddenly find football players at your table.

This first recipe came out in wartime England, and I wish I had a nickel for every time I've copied it for people, and for each one I've made for a bake sale, because I'd be rich. Never make only one—they keep "as long as permitted," which is the way one dear old lady of my acquaintance described the keeping property of a recipe she was giving me, depending on how many teenage boys and others you have in the house. You don't need to freeze it, just keep it in an airtight container—they "mature" like fine wine. I never make fewer than 12 at a time—which is the number of pans of the required size I have.

Oaten Shortbread

1 ¼ cups quick cooking oats
½ cup flour
⅓ cup sugar
¾ stick butter or margarine

Mix dry ingredients together. Rub in butter or margarine. Grease 8-inch cake pan. Press mixture into pan. Bake at 375° until light golden brown (about 17 to 20 minutes). Cut while still warm into wedge shaped pieces. Leave in pan until cold.

If your family really likes things with oats try Oatmeal Cookies.

Oatmeal Cookies

1 cup soft shortening
1 cup brown sugar
½ cup sugar
1 egg

Place shortening, sugar, egg,
beat thoroughly. Sift together flour, salt and soda; add to shortening mixture, mixing well. Blend in oats and drop by teaspoons onto greased cookie sheets. Bake in moderate oven (350°) 12 to 15 minutes.

Ever popular are Toll House Cookies.

Toll House Cookies

2 ¼ cups sifted flour
1 teaspoon baking soda
1 teaspoon salt
1 cup butter or margarine
¾ cup white sugar
¾ cup brown sugar (packed)
1 teaspoon vanilla
½ teaspoon water
2 eggs
12 ounces semi-sweet chocolate ships
1 cup coarsely chopped walnuts

Sift together flour, baking soda and salt. Set aside. Blend butter or margarine and sugar, vanilla and water. Beat in eggs. Add flour mixture and mix well. Stir in chocolate chips and nuts. Drop by half teaspoonfuls on greased cookie sheet. Bake at 375° for 10 to 12 minutes.

Chocolate Covered Orange Balls

1 pound confectioners sugar
1 box vanilla wafers (12 ounces), crushed
1 cup finely chopped walnuts
½ stick soft butter
1 small can (6 ounces) frozen orange juice, thawed, undiluted
1 ½ pounds semi-sweet chocolate chips (two packages), melted

Put all the ingredients except the chocolate into a large bowl. Mix well. Shape into small balls the size of a walnut. Let dry about an hour. Melt the chocolate in a double boiler over low heat. Dip the balls in the melted chocolate to coat. Let dry on cookie sheet, then place into holiday cups.

This last cookie is our family favorite. It is as good as any of the German or Scandinavian butter cookies you may have had and is a lot easier to make.

Berfro Cakes (Welsh Shortbread Cookies)

2 ounces sugar
4 ounces (1 stick) butter
6 ounces flour

Put all ingredients into a bowl and rub the fat into the dry ingredients with your fingers. Do not use a food processor. Mix very thoroughly. Roll into a long roll and slice off thin slices. Bake on a greased cookie sheet in a moderate oven (375°) for about seven minutes until a light golden brown. Alternatively, you can put the roll, wrapped in foil or waxed paper, into the refrigerator and cook at a later time. If the dough is too cold it may crumble on cutting—if so, just leave it at room temperature for a while. I never make a single batch of these either. These will also keep "as long as permitted."

When my husband went to Viet Nam I tucked little boxes of these (his favorite) cookies into nooks and crannies in his suitcase. I also sent a small box to a U.S. Marine Corps General friend of ours, to his surprise. Well, hasn't it always been traditional to send cookies to the troops?

Now we come to some traditional English desserts that seem to go down just as well in the New World.

Victoria Sponge

1 stick butter
⅔ cup sugar
1 cup self-raising flour
2 eggs
2 tablespoons warm water

then warm

Now this basic cake can be served in

liked it as a "sandwich," which means it was spread with raspberry jam, then whipped cream and then the second sponge put on top. It will only serve about eight this way. I found that the cream always squished out when I tried to cut the sandwich, so I gave the raspberry jam and whipped cream treatment to each half separately and this way it easily serves twelve. I was once asked for this recipe by a friend who used frozen raspberries instead of the jam and an instant "whipped cream" out of a can and couldn't understand why it didn't taste like the original. However, I do think you could do the same sort of dessert using a yellow cake mix instead of the Victoria sponge base.

Another way to serve this cake is with a butter icing.

Butter Icing

1 stick butter
1 ½ cups sifted confectioners sugar

Cream butter until very soft. Add confectioners sugar gradually, beating well. Add one teaspoon vanilla or other flavoring or instant coffee if desired. Either frost the layers separately or make a sandwich.

I really think the cake mix manufacturers do a wonderful job helping us to make delicious cakes. I do feel that a homemade frosting really makes a big difference and here is a recipe that is easy to make, easy to work with, is versatile and never fails.

Basic Frosting

12 ounces confectioners sugar
2 sticks butter or margarine
⅓ to ½ cup evaporated milk
½ cup cocoa powder or
1 teaspoon vanilla or
1 teaspoon instant coffee

cocoa and the coffee. This is not a cheap frosting
it enough, it comes out light and creamy like the very best Continental Bakery frostings. If you think all your guests will be on a diet and asking for "just a sliver," frost the layers separately—it will make them easier to serve and it is easier to cut one short fat piece than one tall thin slice. It will look just as impressive when you bring them to the table to have two single layer cakes as one two layer cake. And if you only use one, you can pop the other one in the freezer for some other time.

One day my husband called to say that he was bringing some visiting colleagues home for dinner. I quickly worked out what to have, until I got to the dessert and I just hadn't decided. I was crumbling some stale cake doughnuts into a bowl to put them out for the birds when the light dawned and I decided I would use them to make

Classic English Trifle

Some stale cake doughnuts, lady fingers, yellow cake or a Victoria sponge
¼ cup or so sweet sherry
1 pint custard (you can use vanilla pudding using slightly less milk (2 tablespoons) than usual plus a beaten egg
1 package frozen raspberries (or fresh if available)
½ pint whipping cream
Almonds for garnish

Crumble the cake into the bottom of the bowl you are going to serve the trifle in—if possible, glass, because it looks prettiest—it doesn't taste any different. Pour the sherry over the cake. Spread the raspberries over the cake. Make the custard or vanilla pudding and pour over the cake and raspberry mixture. Put a piece of wax paper or plastic wrap on the top of the custard to prevent a skin from forming. Refrigerate. All this can be done in the morning or the day before. When ready to serve, whip the cream, spread it evenly over the custard. Decorate with almonds or other nuts.

I served this delicious trifle and one of the ladies present asked for the recipe. Before I could say anything my teenage son said "First you take some old, stale doughnuts…" All eyes turned on me, not believing, but I decided to own up and said "That's right, folks." Of course you don't have to have stale doughnuts, but if you have them, use them. Usually I have a couple of Victoria sponges in the freezer ready for use, but I have also used old yellow cup cakes.

Now, while that is the classic English trifle, in these days of not wanting to waste a thing you can adapt the basic principle to other things. I have made a very delicious dessert using gingerbread and applesauce instead of the sponge and raspberries. You can also use up chocolate cake using nuts instead of fruit (unless you happen to like the German combination of chocolate and cherries, in which case you could use them) and chocolate pudding instead of the custard. And the cream on top, of course.

... for guests is gingerbread and applesauce served with ... left over it can go into the freezer ... above.

6

Lunch or Supper

own if they don't. [illegible]
are so busy and important they just never have a spare [illegible]
are visiting the area and you desperately want to see them and didn't get the word about the visit until all the evening meals were spoken for, then—you just may have to give a lunch. So here are a few recipes for easy but elegant meals.

Quiche—or Ham And Egg Pie

1 unbaked 8-inch or 9-inch pie shell
½ cup diced ham
2 eggs
1 ¼ cups milk
1 tablespoon onion flakes
1 cup grated cheese
1 teaspoon dried parsley
¼ teaspoon tarragon
¼ teaspoon thyme
⅛ teaspoon black pepper
⅛ teaspoon salt

Spread ham over bottom of pie shell, then the grated cheese. Beat the eggs with the milk. Add the rest of the ingredients. Pour over the ham and cheese in the pastry case. Bake at 350° for approximately 45 minutes, or until mixture is set and pale and golden brown on top. As this serves six you will need two if you have twelve people.

The great thing about this dish is that it is just as good cold as it is hot, so you can have it in the summer cold and in winter hot. Serve with a tossed salad and fruit for dessert. You can make a pile of pastry cases and keep them in the freezer which makes this a much more possible spur of the moment meal.

This next dish is my husband's favorite food—he would rather have it than steak. But then, he has an unusual palate.

Salmon Bisque

Three 1-pound cans of red salmon
3 cups canned tomatoes or six large tomatoes, skinned
1 cup chopped onion
6 tablespoons chopped parsley or celery leaves

water into a pa...
mering, melt the butter in a saucep...
blended. Slowly add the milk, stirring constantly. Add th...
and paprika. When the sauce is smooth and boiling, strain the salmon mixture and add it to the sauce. Do not allow the bisque to boil. Serve at once—or, it freezes very well so can be made ahead of time, but defrost thoroughly before reheating and do not allow it to boil.

This is good served with English muffins, or scones. It is also excellent with Bran Oatmeal Muffins.

Bran Oatmeal Muffins

2 cups boiling water
2 cups 100% bran cereal
1 cup shortening
2 cups white or brown sugar
4 eggs
1 quart buttermilk
5 cups flour
1 teaspoon salt
5 teaspoons baking soda
4 cups uncooked oatmeal
Raisins or dates, if desired

Pour boiling water over the bran and set aside. Cream sugar and shortening. Add eggs, buttermilk, flour, salt and soda. Add cereals last. Pour into well greased or paper lined muffin tins until ¾ full. Bake in preheated oven 375 degrees for 15 to 20 minutes.

This batter can be refrigerated for later use. Add raisins etc. just before baking. Bake 20 to 25 minutes if just out of the refrigerator.

Serve with a tossed salad and fruit, or on a really hot day, lime sherbet with apricot nectar poured over it.

Now we come to another family favorite. All of these luncheon dishes are very popular with my family for an evening meal and could just as easily be served for Sunday supper for guests.

Quick Macaroni Tuna Bake

1 pound package macaroni, cooked
2 cans tuna (7 ounces each)
2 cans condensed cream of mushroom soup
[illegible] soup cans full of milk

Add cooked ma[illegible]
mix or buttered breadcrumbs. Bake a[illegible]
This makes a large casserole. You can cook it in two [illegible]
ones, in which case you will see it divides very neatly into one can tuna, one can mushroom soup, ¾ can milk, ¼ cup sour cream and half the macaroni in each one.

Again, all that is needed is a tossed salad and fruit for dessert.

I have given you the recipe for Beef Stroganoff as invented for the Czars. Now here is an equally good peasant version you could serve for lunch or supper.

Hamburger Stroganoff

2 pounds ground round or chuck
1 can cream of chicken soup
½ cup sour cream
1 pound mushrooms, peeled and cut into large pieces,
2 cups sliced onions
3 tablespoons corn oil

Cook onions in corn oil until just transparent. Add mushrooms and cook a little longer. Remove from heat and add cream of chicken soup and sour cream. Brown meat in separate skillet—there should be enough fat in the meat not to need any added. Drain and add to other ingredients. Serve with boiled rice or noodles.

I once got myself into the position of giving a wedding lunch for 150 people. I had said I would give a reception for 50—thinking in terms of punch and cake in the middle of the afternoon. But the couple misunderstood, I guess, because they sent out 50 invitations and then things escalated from there. And as it turned out to be a morning wedding, people arrived at our house just at lunch time, so I felt obliged to offer a meal. I decided on chicken salad and if I can give it to 150 people you should have no trouble at all with a mere dozen or so! In case you are interested, for 150 people you need 50 pounds of chicken, 250 rolls, six iceberg lettuces (people tend to think it is just a decoration, so not much gets eaten), six boxes cherry tomatoes, a pound of coffee and a pint of cream.

Chicken Salad

2 cups cooked diced chicken
1 cup chopped celery
½ cup seedless green grapes
[illegible]yonnaise

[illegible]easoning, if nec-

The nice thing about serving this dish is that it can be rea[illegible] day before and combined just before you are ready to serve. Even the celery can be chopped up ahead of time and stored in a plastic container or bag. As this is essentially a warm weather menu, be sure to keep it well refrigerated until serving time.

As it is a warm weather dish try serving a fresh fruit salad with a spot of lemon sherbet in it for dessert. This is one place where I will recommend that you serve some kind of roll or biscuit. Add a tossed salad and some fruit to follow.

You could, of course, serve any of the dishes suggested for dinner to your luncheon guests, but cut down on the "go with"—a tossed salad instead of vegetables, and skip the starter. In these days of everyone on a diet, most people just can't eat two big meals in a day and lunch has traditionally been the lighter of the two, although from a health point of view it is better to have the main meal in the middle of the day and a light meal in the evening. No matter, we have to stick to the prevailing customs.

Having said I don't give lunches if I can avoid it, my family says I should own up and admit that on two different occasions, for a period of a year each time, each Sunday after Quaker Meeting I invited an indefinite number of people home for lunch. My family nicknamed them "The Lunch Bunch." It wasn't planned at all, it just sort of grew, like Topsy. I started by inviting a young Navy man who lived in the barracks and then his friend and then some other young people from the Meeting to meet them and so it grew. Then I decided I should include some of the older members of the Meeting to try and break down the "generation gap" although I must say I've never really experienced it myself. And so each Sunday there would be from two to 20 extra people around the table.

In the beginning I just made sure I had some sandwich makings in the house and some cans of soup I could open. As we were living in a resort area and I passed a grocery store on the way home, if I had invited more people than was prudent for the number of provisions in the house I could stop at the store for, say, extra milk on the way home. But the second year I did it, this wasn't possible, although the group tended to vary in size much less and so it was easier to plan.

I soon found that making sandwiches "to order" for 20 or so people was quite a chore and took a lot of time, so one Sunday I had lasagna. Then it went on from there. Actually it was an act of faith, because somehow the number of people coming home always seemed to match up with the amount of food available. I reasoned if Jesus could feed 5,000 with just five loaves and two fishes I should be able to do all right with a well stocked freezer and larder at my disposal. Somehow it always worked but I can't tell you how to plan for it, because I didn't myself.

7

Preserves and Chutneys

chapters. Here

Strawberry Jam

2 quarts strawberries (5 cups crushed fruit)
3 pounds sugar (7 cups)
1 box Sure-Jell
½ teaspoon butter

Remove caps from berries. Crush berries, one layer at a time. Have measured sugar ready. Add Sure-Jell and butter to fruit in large saucepan and bring to a full rolling boil over high heat, stirring constantly. Quickly add sugar, all at once. Bring to a full rolling boil and continue boiling for one minute, stirring constantly. Skim off any foam with a metal spoon. Pour into warm jars immediately and seal with paraffin, then metal lid. Makes seven cups

Berry Jam

Raspberries, blackberries, loganberries, ollalieberries all can be substituted for the strawberries. Follow procedure as for strawberry jam, above.

Grape Jelly

3 ½ pounds Concord grapes
3 pounds sugar (7 cups)
1 ½ cups water
1 packet Sure-Jell
½ teaspoon butter

Remove grapes from stems. Thoroughly crush fruit, one layer at a time. Place in large saucepan, add water. Bring to a boil: cover and simmer ten minutes, stirring occasionally. Extract juice by placing in a jelly bag, and let it drip (it may take up to four hours). If you don't have a jelly bag you can tie the fruit in unbleached muslin, or similar cloth.

When dripping has almost ceased, to speed up the extraction, gently squeeze bag. Measure five cups of juice. Have sugar ready. Add Sure-Jell and butter to measured juice. Bring to a full rolling boil over high heat. Immediately stir in sugar. Bring to a full rolling boil and boil one minute, stirring constantly. Pour into warm jars. Seal with paraffin and metal lid. Makes about eight cups. This Grape Jelly doesn't taste like any grape jelly you have ever had.

This next is somewhat like Major Grey's Chutney, only better, so I gave it a promotion. My husband said, "I didn't have anything to do with it." My reply was that he didn't think Major Grey had anything to do with his chutney, did he? It was his cook. Well, this one is from Colonel Coile's cook.

Coile's Chutney

1 lemon
4 teaspoons curry powde
2 teaspoons salt
½ pound dark brown sugar
¼ pint syrup from canned fruit

Peel bananas, which should be as ripe as possible. Cut into small pieces. Add dates to bananas in saucepan. Chop lemon very fine, being sure to save juice. Pour in vinegar. Cover pan and simmer for about 1 ½ hours until bananas are soft. Stir in chopped ginger, salt, curry powder, raisins, sugar and fruit syrup. Cook, uncovered, until thickened, about 30 minutes. Stir often. Pour into warm jars and seal.

*If you are using fresh root ginger, add to dates and bananas.

Cranberry Port Chutney

1 ½ cups port
1 ¼ cups sugar
1 orange, chopped zest and juice
¼ cups currants
¼ cup golden raisins
¼ cup dried cranberries
¼ cup dried cherries
1 package fresh cranberries

Heat the port, sugar, orange juice and zest, currants, golden raisins, dried cranberries and dried cherries in a saucepan and bring to a boil. Turn down heat and simmer for five minutes. Add the fresh cranberries and cook until they split open, about another five minutes. Pack in jars and store in a cool, dark place.

Once I made this we have never had any other kind of cranberry sauce or relish. We use it with turkey and chicken, and with pork stroganoff. We also use it to make tea sandwiches with cream cheese.

8

Candies

candy w

recipes for you to try.

I think I must have copied out

any others. These three candies are easy and fool

good not only for home consumption but are good for the tim

you are asked for something for a bake sale and also make good gifts.

I must have made hundreds of pounds of this fudge. Everyone says it is the best they have ever tasted. It is very easy, and this recipe makes a lot, so you can take care of your gift giving in a hurry. Or make a lot of money for the bake sale.

Fabulous Fudge

2 pounds sugar (4 ½ cups)
Pinch of Salt
1 tablespoon butter (1 ounce)
14 ounce can evaporated milk
12 ounces semi-sweet chocolate chips
12 ounces unsweetened chocolate, chopped small
1 pint marshmallow cream
2 cups chopped walnuts

Boil the sugar, salt, butter and milk in a saucepan for six minutes. Put the marshmallow cream and the chocolate in a large bowl. Pour the boiling syrup over them. Beat until chocolate is melted. Stir in nuts. Pour into a shallow pan and spread evenly. Let stand a few hours before cutting. Store in an airtight container in a cool place.

Hint: the marshmallow comes out of the jar more easily if you put it, uncovered, in the microwave for 20 to 30 seconds. Also, I find this fudge easiest to cut with a pizza cutter.

Peanut Brittle

1 cup corn syrup
½ cup light molasses
½ cup sugar
4 tablespoons butter

Combine above ingredients in heavy saucepan. Stir to dissolve sugar. Cook to soft ball stage 238° on candy thermometer. Add two cups salted peanuts. Cook to light crack state 270 to 280°, stirring constantly. Remove from heat, add ½ teaspoon baking soda, and stir lightly. Pour evenly over well greased (with butter) cookie sheet. Spread thin. Let cool. Break into pieces. Makes about 1 ½ pounds.

Sugar Plums

½ cup (1 stick) butter
confectioners sugar, unsifted
eam

heat-

12 ounces semi-sweet chocolate chips
1 teaspoon instant coffee
3 tablespoons butter

Melt above ingredients in double boiler, slowly. Take from heat and add l teaspoon vanilla, one cup (less 2 tablespoons) Eagle Brand condensed milk. Mix well. Refrigerate over night, covered. Take ½ teaspoon of mixture and roll into balls and then roll in chocolate jimmies or cocoa powder.

9

Tea

First, some expla
black tea and Chinese for gre
and garbage"—you know, mint or cha
lemon peel added. My daughter likes all of them, an
mint and chamomile for her.

Tea, not Coke, is the pause that refreshes. Some people say the British Empire ran on tea. If you watch the B.B.C. you will notice people are always drinking tea, or saying "I'll put the kettle on," shorthand for "I'll make a pot of tea." And it should be a pot—even if you are using tea bags, put them in a teapot—much more enticing than a bag in your teacup. Anyway, you can't put the milk in first if you have the teabag in there.

Black tea needs milk, and maybe a little sugar. Milk should be whole milk, not cream and not skim or 2% milk. The milk should be put in the cup first and there is a scientific explanation for this, something to do with milk being an emulsion that reacts differently when added to a hot liquid or a hot liquid being added to it. My husband says it is all imagination and is just the "English Tea Ceremony." Could be. But some traditions are worth preserving. Green tea needs nothing added. I never put lemon in tea, but it probably is fine in weeds and garbage.

"Tea" is not only a drink; in England it is a meal, which needs a definition. When restaurants and hotels in America put on a tea, they usually call it "High Tea." In my experience it never is. They probably think it sounds more "up market" than afternoon tea, when the reverse is true. It is always "afternoon tea"—a meal that was invented by the aristocracy to bridge the void between lunch at noon and dinner at eight, so is served at 4 o'clock.

Afternoon tea consists of small sandwiches, cakes, cookies and maybe fruit, especially strawberries, served with cream. It can be informal—a cup of tea and a cookie as served mid-afternoon in English workplaces, including offices, or if a friend drops by. Or it can be a very elaborate affair.

"High Tea" is a much more substantial meal and always includes something cooked—a boiled egg, poached or scrambled eggs on toast, sardines on toast, a nice kipper, an omelet or perhaps a salad. This is served about 5 o'clock to the children in the nursery, or at about 6 o'clock to the breadwinners in the family when they come home from work. They have traditionally eaten “dinner” at noon, maybe in a work’s canteen.

Although we still have dinner parties, once a year we have an open
... in the form of “Tea in the Garden.” There is a great mystique
... people love to come. Most of the menu can be made
... nth. We have over 100 guests. The great
... no alcohol (except in the tri-

... eone to

an ...
the dishes.

This chapter is dedica...
whom it would not be possible:

Jude Bolon
Edie Maruyama
Averil Nero
Margaret Chung Prodis
Joanne Ryder
Rita Stiny
Pat Turner
Joy Erler Weyer
my daughter Jennifer
daughter-in-law Lori Coile
and granddaughter Sienna Coile Robrock

Menu for Tea in the Garden

Tea sandwiches:

Smoked Salmon

Cucumber

Cheddar Cheese and Colonel Coile's Chutney

Cream Cheese and Cranberry Port Chutney

[illegible] ilities: ham, chicken, turkey)

Scones with whipped butter and homemade jam (strawberry is traditional)

Cookies:

Toll House

Coconut

Oaten Shortbread

Berfro Cakes (Welsh shortbread)

Cheese Wafers

Chocolate Orange Balls

Strawberries and Cream

Trifle

Rum Cake

See recipe under "desserts."

Tea Time Fruit Cake is a light fruit cake—a cake with fruit, not like the American version that is fruit with a small amount of cake to bind it together.

Tea Time Fruit Cake

1 cup butter
2 cups sugar
2 eggs
1 cup sour cream
½ teaspoon vanilla
2 cups (10 ½ ounces) flour
1 teaspoon baking powder
¼ teaspoon salt
1 cup chopped walnuts (or any kind of nuts)
½ cup raisins
½ cup glace cherries

Preheat oven to 350°. Cream butter and sugar until very light and fluffy. Beat in eggs, one at a time, until well blended. Fold in sour cream and vanilla. Mix the flour, baking powder and salt and add the nuts, cherries and raisins. Mix well until the fruit is well coated with the flour. Add to the butter mixture: mix well. pour into a well-greased and floured bundt pan or a 9-inch tube pan. Bake at 350° for about an hour or until golden brown and cake tester comes out clean. Cool on rack before handling.

Shortcake Almondine

Crust:

cups (11 ¼ ounces) flour

1 teaspoon

1 egg, lightly beaten

4 whole almonds

Heat oven to 325°. Grease 10-inch or 9-inch springform pan. Lightly spoon flour into measuring cup, level off in large bowl (if weighing, put flour in bowl and stir with a wire whisk). Blend all crust ingredients at lowest speed until dough forms. Chill, if desired. Divide dough in half, spread half in bottom of prepared pan. In small bowl blend all filling ingredients except whole almonds. Spread over crust to within ½ inch of side of pan. Press remaining dough to 10-inch or 9-inch circle on wax paper, place dough over filling, paper side up. Remove waxed paper, press dough into place. Garnish with almonds. Bake at 325° for 45 to 55 minutes or until light golden brown. Cool 15 minutes. Remove from pan. Cool completely. 24 to 32 servings. Note: If you do not like marzipan you will not like this cake.

Chocolatissimo

10 ounces semisweet chocolate (10 squares or 1 ⅔ cups pieces)
1 ¼ cups sugar
1 teaspoon instant coffee
1 ¼ cups (10 ounces) butter
10 eggs, separated

Melt chocolate with coffee in top of double boiler or bowl set over hot, not boiling water. Stir until smooth: cool. Cream butter and sugar in very large bowl. Add chocolate, blend well. Add egg yolks, one at a time, beating well after each addition. Beat for a total of 15 minutes. In another large bowl, with clean beaters, beat egg whites until stiff but not dry. Fold into chocolate mixture. Measure and refrigerate ¼ of the mixture. Pour remainder into greased (bottom only) 9-inch spring form pan. Bake in pre-heated 350° oven 50 minutes. Cool completely in pan on rack. (Cake will sink in the middle. Spread reserved chocolate mixture over top. Cover, chill overnight. If desired, garnish with powdered sugar. Serve in thin slices. Serves 12.

Cream Scones

10 ounces flour
½ teaspoon salt
4 ounces (1 stick) butter
[illegible] baking powder
[illegible] bstitutes

[illegible]

[illegible] until ½-inch thick. Cu[illegible] tered baking sheet. Re-roll dough and cu[illegible] to 12 minutes. Serve with whipped butter and strawberry jam.

Classic English Trifle

See recipe in Chapter 5.

Chocolate Sheet Cake

1 cup (2 sticks butter—8 ounces)
2 cups flour
2 cups sugar
1 cup water
¼ cup cocoa
½ cup buttermilk
2 eggs, beaten
1 teaspoon baking soda
1 teaspoon cinnamon (optional)
1 teaspoon vanilla

Sift together sugar and flour into large bowl. Combine butter, water and cocoa in saucepan and bring to a boil. Pour cocoa mixture over sugar and flour, stir well. Add remaining ingredients. Mix well. Pour into greased and floured 11 x 16 inch cake pan. Bake at 400° for 20 minutes.

Frosting (optional): Combine ½ cup (1 stick, 4 ounces) butter, ¼ cup cocoa and 6 tablespoons milk in saucepan. Bring to a boil. Remove from heat and add one box (1-pound) confectioners sugar and 1 teaspoon vanilla. Beat well. Mix in 1 cup chopped nuts, if desired (or sprinkle on top). Spread on cake while it is still hot from the oven.

I don't serve this at my tea, but it is a useful recipe to have if you are asked to take a dessert to a potluck. Very easy and delicious, with or without frosting.

I am sure you have other tried and true recipes of your own. These are just to get you started and give you an idea of the sort of thing you are aiming for. As long as you use butter in your baking, store things in an air tight container in a cool place, things will keep for a month or so without freezing. I am not a big fan of freezing baked goods—they are never quite right and pastry that has been frozen after baking is like cardboard. Freezing it in an uncooked state improves it. I do all the baking for our Tea in the Garden myself.

My “kitchen crew” comes between noon and one o’clock so th

outside on the back terrace next to the herb garden and all over our front yard. There are other nooks both inside and out with places to sit if people want to be quiet.

The weather will be “gorgeous.” “How do I know?” We live in central California where we have seven months without rain. This may sound wonderful to most people, but the other side of the coin is that it makes it very difficult to grow a garden.

At last—4 o'clock! Everything is under control. We greet people on our front porch as they arrive. We have some sort of music playing. We have had bagpipers and Morris Dancers, a flutist, folk musicians with violin and recorder, a fiddle and dulcimer, and Dixieland Jazz. They have all been great.

People are encouraged to go into the dining room and get some goodies, then into the adjacent kitchen to get a cup of tea. One year one of my helpers came to tell me that a man wanted coffee—could he have some? I said, "No. This is a tea. If I had wanted to have a coffee I would have had it in the morning at 11 o'clock. Sorry."

I have an English garden. Each English garden has a "statement," or theme. I have frogs. I have a lot of them, but as they are tucked away among the plants, it doesn't feel like there are too many. I have one very big frog and many small ones and lots in between. People keep bringing them to me saying, "I saw this and thought of you." Perhaps I should have chosen angels instead. The occasional one expires. As they are not able to earn their keep by eating insects like real ones, I have them to help spread guests around the yard who are participating in a frog counting contest. The three people who come closest to the correct number get a prize, usually a hanging basket of flowers, or an orchid. A lot of people are very enthusiastic, especially children. One year it amused everybody when our Police Chief got the correct number of 167 on the nose. Now there are over 200.

Epilogue

I took a trip to England and my then 21-year-old son decided to give [illegible]
dinner party while I was away. He [illegible]

[illegible] and crackers with the drinks. Chicken Americana. Baked potatoes with sour cream, peas, salad, followed by strawberry ice cream with frozen strawberries.

I am sure you will find entertaining relatively trouble free and easy with this book. Enjoy!

Ellen Miller Coile

Recipe Index

978-0-595-67698-9
0-595-67698-7